Series / Number 02-027

The Impact of Very Small Size on the International Behavior of Microstates

GEORGE L. REID
Ministry of Finance and Planning (Barbados)

SAGE PUBLICATIONS / Beverly Hills / London

For information address:

SAGE PUBLICATIONS, INC.
275 South Beverly Drive
Beverly Hills, California 90212

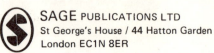

SAGE PUBLICATIONS LTD
St George's House / 44 Hatton Garden
London EC1N 8ER

International Standard Book Number **0-8039-0406-1**

Library of Congress Catalog Card No. L.C. 74-78046

FIRST PRINTING

When citing a professional paper, please use the proper form. Remember to cite the correct Sage Professional Paper series title and include the paper number. One of the two following formats can be adapted (depending on the style manual used):

(1) AZAR, E. E. (1972) "International Events Interaction Analysis." Sage Professional Papers in International Studies, 1, 02-001. Beverly Hills and London: Sage Pubns.

OR

(2) Azar, Edward E. 1972. *International Events Interaction Analysis.* Sage Professional Papers in International Studies, Vol. 1., no. 02-001. Beverly Hills and London: Sage Publications.

CONTENTS

The Impact of Very Small Size on the International Behavior of Microstates

GEORGE L. REID
Ministry of Finance and Planning (Barbados)

This paper focuses on certain aspects of the international behavior of very small states. The issues to which it directs attention have become prominent with the accession to political independence of many very small states in the period since 1960. The search for political independence by such miniscule communities can be regarded as an indication of the fluidity of the norms which underpin the contemporary international system. Indeed, it can be inferred from the emergence of very small entities as independent nations that criteria of statehood and concepts of viability have undergone a major change. At the same time, it should be recognized that the trend toward the attainment of statehood by smaller political communities comes at a time when many larger states are moving toward a process of integration. The latter trend, which is particularly noticeable in Western Europe, indicates an awareness by political leaders, in the more advanced countries of the world, that technological change has brought the viability of the traditional nation-state into question. As

AUTHOR'S NOTE: *This monograph is based on a thesis submitted for the Ph.D. degree of the University of Southampton, England. I am especially indebted to Professor Joseph Frankel, my teacher, for his encouragement and guidance. I must also thank Joseph M. Scolnick, Jr. for his helpful comments and criticism of earlier versions of this paper. Neither of these persons, of course, is in any way responsible for the shortcomings of the present text.*

Harold and Margaret Sprout (1968) have suggested, such a trend can be interpreted as a response by political leaders to domestic constituency pressures for improvements in domestic welfare. Thus, it can be argued that the acceptance of multinational solutions to the problem of achieving and sustaining a high level of economic growth implies some downgrading in the importance of political sovereignty.

If the period since the mid-1950s appears as one of integration for Western European communities, it has also been the heyday of a new type of territorial state which has risen from the ruins of Western European colonial empires. Decolonization, the dominant theme of this period, has resulted in the emergence of a plethora of new states. As the tide of decolonization has moved on apace, leaving the hard-core areas of Southern Africa as the last stronghold of resistance, attention has turned increasingly to the very small territories, many of which are island remnants of empires. The more fervent anticolonialists insist that the principles enshrined in United Nations General Assembly Resolution 1514 (XV), which contains the Declaration on the *Granting of Independence to Colonial Countries and Peoples,* are equally applicable to these territories. Their critics point out that some of these very small territories present unique problems of decolonization due to their general lack of human and material resources and, in many cases, to their geographic isolation. Even if a more sanguine approach would suggest that pragmatic modalities of self-determination should be fashioned to suit the needs of these countries, in the absence of any satisfactory alternative, decolonization may boil down to granting them a more or less separate independence.

Scholarly interest in analysis of the problems of microstates seems to be directly related to the growing membership of these states in the contemporary international system. Attention has been given to such issues as the effect of microstate membership on the functioning of the United Nations (Harris, 1970). The question of the viability of very small states and whether minute size is a major hindrance to growth and development has been discussed in a general way (Benedict, 1967; de Smith, 1970; Rapoport, 1971). However, little research has been devoted to the external behavior of very small states. The execution of such research can be facilitated by the development of an appropriate methodology and the explicit formulation of hypotheses which are amenable to verification by empirical evidence.

The study of the problems of microstates raises issues which are of central concern to all students of international politics and foreign policy. On the one hand, the emergence of these miniscule entities emphasizes the need for a continuing examination of the modalities of change and stability in the contemporary international system. On the other, it points to the need for a reexamination of the role of some of the traditional instruments of statecraft. Further, a comparison between microstates and larger actors in contemporary world affairs will emphasize the lack of congruence between formal legal notions about the equality of states and their capabilities. From the viewpoint of foreign policy analysis, a focus on microstates can illuminate the central process of formulation and execution of undertakings aimed at preserving or altering some aspect of the external environment. Microstate political structures can be expected to be less complex than those of larger states, thereby allowing key elements in decision-making to be more easily identified.

The setting up of a taxonomy which distinguishes microstates as a separate class allows generalizations to be framed about characteristic patterns of their behavior. Kegley (1973) has argued that the development of general theoretical statements about foreign policy behavior is dependent upon the construction of an empirical typology of the external behavior of nations which could serve as an instrument for comparing and measuring cross-national variations. It seems that the categories within such a typology could be expected to be associated with a large number of determinants or causal variables. In order to measure such relationships effectively, a prior classification of states according to the determinants of their behavior is necessary.

An approach of this type is relatively new. Indeed, the predominant form of analysis of foreign policy behavior has concentrated on individual countries. An approach which places its emphasis on the individual country is of very limited usefulness for the understanding of the nature of foreign policy in general. With the rapid increase in the membership of the international community, has come a marked increase in the differences between individual states. States in the contemporary system differ not only in size, but also in resources, capabilities, ideological underpinnings, and levels of political, social and economic development.

The existence of significant differences between states presents a major challenge to the formulation of valid generalizations about foreign policy. It would seem that a comparative approach offers the most promising prospect for the generation of useful insights. Unfortunately, little work has been done with the specific objective of developing comparative concepts for organizing research on international behavior. Clearly, a first approach is to establish useful classifications which distinguish states in a number of dimensions. The lack of satisfaction with the criteria on which classifications in the contemporary literature have been based has been most aptly expressed by one writer (Rosenbaum, 1970: 617) who has pointed out that although it is now recognized that the bases of power are widely distributed and varied, the classification of states in terms of the categories super power, middle power, small power, and micro power, do no more than express an implicit notion about what would happen if World War II should occur again.

The construction of appropriate taxonomies could facilitate the development of coordinated studies of foreign policy processes in different kinds of states. Generalizations which describe foreign policy behavior could be tested to discover their validity for all classes of states. At least one outcome of such studies could be to focus attention on whether there is a central element in the behavior of all classes of states to which the descriptive term foreign policy can be applied. In recent studies, scholars like McClelland (1972: 27) have claimed that there exist different types of "foreign policy outputs," and that for comparative purposes it is essential to discover which linked domestic or intrapolity processes are associated regularly with which types of foreign policy outputs. McClelland suggests, therefore, that a classification scheme for foreign policy outputs could be built from the study of the flow of acts directed abroad by the polity.

Other writers who have been concerned with the problem of policy classification (Hermann, 1972: 58-79) have recognized that for their taxonomic schemes to be useful, they must offer theoretically relevant ways of identifying different kinds of policies. They have argued, however, that the critical weakness which is faced by classification schemes is the absence of well-defined foreign policy variables. Noting that many classifications act as organizing devices but that satisfactory fulfilment of this function does not necessarily give rise to the generation of theory, they have claimed that many studies of foreign policy have stopped short at classification. They have argued, therefore, that an interest in scientific theory will require that an appropriate classification scheme identify significant relationships and provide instruments for measuring these relationships.

It is undeniable that the establishment of appropriate schemes along which actors and their behavior can be classified is a major prerequisite for comparative analysis of foreign policy activity. From a methodological point of view, the broad requirements of useful classification schemes can be identified. However, it is hardly possible to specify rules to insure that the particular system which is advocated will assist in the development of theory. In any event, the choice of a particular taxonomic scheme usually involves personal evaluations which are often not directly related to the research tasks of the scholar.

Although in this paper we will focus on size as a major independent variable[1] in patterns of foreign policy behavior, it is likely that many other variables may have more potent effects on foreign policy behavior in specific situations than mere size. What must be noted is that while many of the other factors underlying a state's external behavior can undergo a significant degree of change, size, in terms of relative endowment of resources of states, is a more or less permanent feature. Indeed, the size of a state can limit the magnitude of possible change of other variables such as political, social, and economic development. The existence of such a relationship suggests the need for analytical strategies which treat size as the primary independent variable, with other important attributes of states as secondary independent variables.

A number of studies which explore the impact of specific independent variables on foreign policy are now being carried out, and preliminary results of them are available (Salmore and Hermann, 1969: East, 1973; Hermann and East, 1972). Size, economic development, and political accountability are the three independent variables on which attention has been focused. The major working assumption of some of the studies has been that the effect of each independent variable is additive, and that each one has an impact on foreign policy behavior independent of the other two properties. An important conclusion which has been derived from these studies is that while the physical size of a nation appears to be the most potent of the three national attributes in accounting for foreign policy behavior, political accountability is of crucial significance.

The studies mentioned above have been faced with the necessity of avoiding a priori decisions about what types of external behavior should be the focus of their investigations. They have been concerned with the application of systematic operational procedures which permit analysis of a wide range of behavior. Since their approach is a comparative one, these studies have used schemes which permit the coding and classification of data representative of the behavior of a large number of nation states. The approach of the present paper is pre-empirical in that it does not advocate a specific scheme for collecting and manipulating data on the external behavior of very small states. Rather, it addresses itself to the problem of definition and identification of microstates, and discusses a number of factors which account for their general foreign policy orientations. However, this approach does follow the current trend toward the development of a scientific study of foreign policy in that it generates a number of hypotheses about the impact of very small size on foreign policy behavior. At a future date, the author hopes to collect hard data against which the hypotheses can be tested. In a latter section of this paper a preliminary discussion will be given on the methodology which could be used for collecting the necessary data. However, at this juncture it seems necessary to specify our concept of "microstate."

MICROSTATE AS AN ANALYTICAL CONCEPT

A major difficulty frequently encountered in analytical writing is that which arises from the necessity of using terms which are part of everyday language. In conventional discussion, the term "microstate" appears to convey the notion that the entities which are so described differ significantly from those to which the term "state" is usually applied. A good example of the way in which the term has been used to convey this distinction can be found in a document prepared by the Secretary-General of the United Nations. This document (U.N. Doc. A/6701/Add. 1, 1967) describes microstates as "entities which are exceptionally small in area, population and human and economic resources, and which are now emerging as independent States." While the definition specifies the variables on which a classification of microstates can be established, its usefulness is limited by its failure to indicate the parameters which circumscribe the notion of extreme smallness. As a result, it would be of little assistance in the construction of a list of microstates.

In locating microstates within a taxonomic scheme dichotomizing the contemporary international system according to a typology of national actors which is both mutually exclusive and exhaustive, we must dispose of a number of specific problems. Ideally, our scheme should partition states into classes which are so constructed that members of a given class are more similar to each other in terms of a number of selected attributes than they are to members of other classes. In sum, as Burgess (1970) has pointed out, an effective system of classification must minimize within-class variance while maximizing between-class variance with respect to the indices on which the typology is based. He has advocated the use of discriminant analysis as a statistical technique for partitioning the set of variables which are used in such a way as to minimize the number of misclassifications and maximize the distance between the resulting groupings.

An alternative technique for constructing classifications of states is that of hierarchical clustering which has been suggested by Johnson (1967) and discussed by Taylor (in Rapoport, 1971) with particular reference to its usefulness in separating microstates from other classes of states. The technique is essentially one of compiling a matrix of distances between states, in terms of a number of selected variables, and regarding those states whose distances fall within a specific limit as comprising a particular class.

Microstates might be identified by ranking all states which are members of the contemporary international system according to a number of selected attributes and regarding those which are lowest ranked as microstates. Such an approach would require that a prior decision be made about the attributes on which states should be ranked. Vayrynen (1971) has suggested that measures of rank may be distinguished as objective or subjective according to whether the indicators on which the measures are based are "hard" aggregate data, such as total land area, population, Gross National Product, and so on, or whether the indicator describes perceptions. He has suggested, also, that a further distinction can be made between *endogenous* measures which describe properties internal to the actor, and *exogenous* measures whose referents are external judgements.

It should be recognized that the various types of measures of a state's rank are interrelated. Judgments and perceptions must be based on objective phenomena. At the same time, the measurement process itself is subjective since the effort to measure social phenomena involves inferences which may vary from observer to observer. The point to be borne in mind is that the study of international behavior is the study of patterns of interaction, and interaction depends not only on capabilities, but also on perceptions. However, as Small and Singer (1973) have pointed out in a recent study, the power or capability of a state will certainly affect its score in rankings of diplomatic importance, but the measures which may be compiled are not identical.

The approach which appears to provide the most useful point of departure for identifying microstates is that of using objective endogenous attributes as measures of rank. As we have noted, such referents include total land area, population, Gross National Product, military expenditures, and so on. These socioeconomic variables are highly interrelated. Thus, if states are ranked within a number of frequency distributions, based on different socioeconomic attributes, though the precise numerical rank of a state may vary according to the indicator which is used, certain states will be found in the same segment of each frequency distribution which is compiled. It should be noted, however, that some states may be low-ranked on one dimension of size, while others may be low-ranked on many. The true microstates are those which are low-ranked on multiple measures of size.

In constructing a classification of microstates, two basic problems must be solved. These problems are: that of selecting the appropriate indicator of size and choosing a cutoff point for partitioning microstates from other classes of states. Ideally, one might wish to combine various indicators of size into a composite score on the basis of which states could then be ranked. Such calculations tend to be cumbersome and provide only a slight refinement over the use of the single variable of population.[2] The approach adopted in this essay is, therefore, that of using total population as the measure of size in the classification of states.

Following Taylor and Hudson (1972) all countries which were formally independent in 1972 were ranked in order of population size. This approach resulted in a list of 147 states. After a careful study of the list of states it was decided to use the cutoff point of total population of 1,000,000 or less to distinguish microstates from other classes of states. While it is recognized that this dichotomization is arbitrary it provided us with twenty-six entities which could be used for manipulative analysis. A list of these states is provided in Appendix B.

The major purpose for setting up a classification of microstates is to select entities which are similar in a number of objective features. The availability of a satisfactory number of cases permits an empirical examination to be carried out on whether deductive propositions about the effect of size on foreign policy behavior hold good for a significant number of those cases. The central focus of this paper is the analysis of the proposition that size is a significant factor in the explanation of patterns of foreign policy behavior. Differences in size of states have been given a prominent role in capability analyses of foreign policy. The general thrust of such analyses is to advance the proposition that the size of a state determines the extent of its domestic resources, and since it is these resources which set limits to the state's capacity to formulate and implement various types of foreign policy undertakings, size is, therefore, a crucial variable in international behavior. It would seem that an examination of the impact of very small size on the resources of microstates is necessary if we are to determine the validity of size as a factor which can explain the external behavior of this class of states.

THE CORRELATES OF MICROSIZE

We have chosen size of population as the variable for an initial operationalization of the concept of the microstate. At the same time, it is relevant to examine the relationship of size to some of the other attributes of statehood. Dealing first with territory, it can be suggested that many states with very small populations also have very small land areas. However, the compilation of a list of states with very small populations will reveal no clear correspondence between size of population and size of territory. As a result, microstates will differ significantly in terms of population density. An examination of tabulations compiled by Taylor and Hudson (1972: 299-302) will reveal that some of the smallest states rank very high in frequency distributions of population density, while others are among the lowest ranked.[3]

Both high and low densities of population can present problems for economic development. A country may be so crowded that its population places great pressures on its natural resources. On the other hand, a thinly spread population will require a greater investment in transportation and communications infrastructure per capita. While one must recognize the existence and implications of differences in population density between microstates, the point which must be recognized is that states in this category will have limited land areas. This feature will be particularly evident in the case of island states. Limited land area usually implies limited natural resources, since natural resources tend to be randomly distributed over the surface of the globe. In turn, where a country has few natural resources its economic base will be fragile. For the very small country, the absence of economies of scale acts as a deterrent to the establishment of a diversified pattern of industries and further exacerbates its economic vulnerability. With a limited range of resources, very small countries will tend to be heavily dependent on international trade to supplement the deficiencies of domestic production. Very often the products which are imported are paid for out of the proceeds from the export of a very limited range of commodities. Any adverse movement in the production of, or the external demand for those commodities, can have dire economic consequences for the very small state.

The effect of the economic disabilities of microstates is to make them highly responsive to events which occur in the external environment. Yet, it would seem that other features of microstate socioeconomic and political systems restrict their capacity to respond positively to external occurrences. The limitations in the economic structure of microstates are likely to be reflected in the resources available to their governments. Although the size of the government, when compared with that of larger states, must be regarded as small, it may be the largest single sector of the economy. This feature derives from the fact that the social dynamics of small scale societies often involve the government in the performance of tasks which are executed by private entrepreneurs in larger societies. In particular, it is commonplace to find governments of very small states playing a leading role in the operation of productive enterprises precisely because private individuals are unwilling to undertake the considerable risks involved.

Governments of microstates tend to be faced, paradoxically, both with a wider scope of activity and narrower budgetary resources than those of larger states. Indeed, because per capita welfare expenditures are high, there are severe restrictions on their capacity to equip and maintain military- and foreign-affairs establishments. The consequence of the latter disability is that while the very small state will be highly dependent on the external environment to achieve its domestic goals, its instrumentalities for manipulating that environment are severely limited.

In traditional analyses of small state behavior, disabilities inherent in small size have been regarded as giving rise to a number of important consequences. It has been held that small states will demonstrate a low level of participation in international affairs and that their foreign policies will demonstrate a status quo orientation. As East (1973) has noted in a recent study of small states, the traditional model of small state behavior suggests that the activities of such states will be narrowly delimited both in geographic and functional scope, and that inter-governmental organizations are the major arena of their external activity. Because of their limited military capabilities, small states are expected to avoid the use of force as a technique of statecraft and to rely, alternatively, on international legal norms. As a corollary, small states are expected to avoid indulging in behavior which will tend to alienate more powerful states. It would seem that if the type of behavior which we have outlined is characteristic of small states it should be even more evident in the activity of microstates. The extent to which such patterns of behavior hold good for microstates should be subject to empirical verification; what should be noted is that there are other factors in the political processes of microstates which are indicative of the relevance of alternative models. This issue will be discussed in some detail in a subsequent section of the paper. It is now essential that an explanation be given of the concept of foreign policy which we have been using in this paper.

DEFINITION OF FOREIGN POLICY

K. J. Holsti (1971) and Charles Hermann (1972) have both recently drawn attention to the fact that there is no agreement in the contemporary literature on the meaning of foreign policy. As Holsti (1971: 174) has noted, there has been a tendency among scholars to assume that the content of foreign policy is self-evident. He suggests, therefore, that in view of the underlying ideas which have informed studies in the foreign policy field, the aggregates of actions by governments over a specified period of time might serve as indicators of foreign policy. However, he expresses reservations that the sum of threats, warnings, reprisals, protests, and various forms of cooperative behavior over a specific time period could be demonstrated to adequately express the key concerns of policy-makers, which may involve problem-solving strategies, objectives, rules, commitments, and interests.

Hermann (1972: 72-5) has also proposed that discrete actions should be used as the basic units of foreign policy analysis. He contends that research on foreign policy is needed which treats policy as an operational concept on which empirical data can be gathered for all nation-states. For him, such a specification would require that the unit of analysis be defined so that it can be reliably identified by any careful analyst and that it occurs with sufficient frequency to permit statistical analysis. Hermann recognizes that by concentrating on discrete actions some meaning is lost if the action is separated from the context and sequence of events of which it is a part. However, he suggests that it is easier to assemble discrete actions into alternative, broader clusters than to decompose a larger unit of analysis.

The emphasis on actions as the basic unit of foreign policy stems from an underlying notion. The assumption is, to paraphrase Rosenau (1968: 222) that such actions result from the efforts of duly constituted officials of the national society to preserve or alter a situation in the international system in such a way that it is consistent with a goal or goals decided upon by them or their predecessors. From this perspective, foreign policy is viewed as purposeful activity directed at an external target by the political leaders of national societies. However, doubts may be cast on the usefulness of this concept for studying the external behavior of microstates.

From the standpoint of analysis of foreign policy as rationally motivated behavior, microstates can be expected to undertake few externally oriented actions, in view of their limited capabilities. Although decision makers might wish to engage in a wide range of activity, capabilities will determine what is actually put into effect. Thus, the student who focuses on the foreign policies of very small political units with limited capabilities may find them performing few actions in the external environment. It is in this context that we can understand Holsti's comment (1971: 174) that "one often looks in vain for the 'foreign policy' of many of the microstates; these little entities appear to be more objects than actors in the system."

It may well be that the attainment of independence by many very small states whose leaders are faced with urgent problems of improving the welfare of their domestic constituents may invalidate traditional notions of foreign policy. As we have noted in an earlier section, very small states tend to be highly dependent on external sources of support. They will be inclined to engage in external activity in order to maintain and increase such support, but their activities have objectives which are ultimately domestic rather than external.

A focus on actions as the unit of analysis of foreign policy permits the gathering of empirical data for systematic study of the behavior of nation states. The collection of such data facilitates the investigation of the relationship between the number and types of actions in which a state engages and the size of its resource base, and thereby allows the researcher to determine the relevance of distinguishing states in terms of size. The compilation of data on the actions of nation-states over a specific time period facilitates the development of a profile of the contemporary international system. However, the task of analysis of these actions requires an investigation of the impact of domestic and external factors on the decisions of the authorities which produce them. This type of analysis can be carried out by looking in turn at the decision-making processes of microstates and at the international system at which their outputs are directed.

MICROSTATE DECISION-MAKING

Since the introduction of the original formulation by Richard Snyder and his associates (Snyder et al., 1954) the concept of foreign policy decision-making has become part of the currency of international relations research as well as an acceptable term in the vocabulary of political actors. The basic working premise of the decision-making approach is that political action is undertaken by concrete and identifiable human beings, and that the way to the understanding of the dynamics of this action is to view the world from the perspective of these human actors. To assist the reconstruction of the world of the actors, the analyst is required to examine their behavior from the central focus of an act of choice of one course of action from among a number of competing alternatives. It is this act of choice which is held to constitute a decision.

The decision-making approach offers a taxonomic scheme for analyzing the major factors involved in the making of foreign policy. There have been many contributions to the literature on decision-making which have had the cumulative effect of improving the original formulation. Frankel (1963: 4-5) introduced the distinction between the psychological and the objective environment of the decision maker to take account of the fact that although non-apperceived elements cannot influence decisions, they may be strategically important for the outcome of the resultant actions and may vitiate expectations. Dissatisfaction with the picture conjured up by the theoretical literature of a conscious and thorough-going examination by officials of all possible outcomes from a given action, against a background of self-consciously articulated notions of those which would maximize their values, led Lindblom (1959: 79-88) to suggest an important modification. Lindblom argues that in practice, limitations of intellectual capacity, information, time and money restrict the operation of the involved process suggested in decision-making theory. Lindblom suggested, as an alternative, that decision makers focus on marginal and incremental comparisons, and the only values which are relevant to choice in particular situations are the incremental or marginal amounts by which one policy appears preferable to the other.

More recently, Etzioni (1968: 249-281) has criticized both the rational comprehensive and the incremental models of decision-making as inadequate for a satisfactory explanation of decisional activity and the facilitation of future attempts at problem-solving. He has suggested that *contextuating* (or fundamental) decisions should be differentiated from *bit* (or item) decisions. A further, and fundamental, distinction has been suggested by Allison (1969) in the use of decision-making models. Pointing out that the model most often used in decision-making analyses is a rational policy model (1969: 694) in terms of which analysts attempt to understand happenings as the more or less purposive acts of unified national governments, Allison suggests two alternative models. These are the organizational process model and the bureaucratic politics model. He notes that in terms of the former, the "acts" and "choices" of the rational policy model are seen as the *outputs* of large organizations, functioning according to certain regular patterns of behavior (1969: 700). From the viewpoint of the latter, events in foreign affairs are understood as *outcomes* of various overlapping bargaining games among players arranged hierarchically in the national government (Allison, 1969: 707).

Despite theoretical refinement, the decision-making taxonomy has provided the basis for little empirical research. The reason for this failure is that not only is the framework inordinately complex, but it furnishes little information on which of the many variables are likely to be the most important in different kinds of decisions (Rosenau 1967: 189-211). However, the decision-making approach still remains an important tool for the study of foreign policy behavior. As McClelland (1972: 15-43) has recently noted, in current studies of foreign policy it tends to appear not as the central concept, but as one of the processes within the polity which contributes to foreign policy activity. It is in this context that it is used in our study of microstate foreign policy behavior.

As we have noted, the model of decision-making which is most often used is the rational policy model. While its appropriateness as an explanation of policy formulation in large states may be questioned in view of its failure to take account of the complexity of bureaucratic politics and the operation of organizational processes, there are other factors which cast doubts on its relevance for the analysis of foreign policy behavior of microstates. Indeed, it seems that the presence of some of the organizational and bureaucratic features of large states which make it less than adequate to the understanding of their political processes, render it, by their absence, too elaborate a characterization of the reality of political activity of microstates. The resource deficiencies, the lack of well-developed structures, and the very limited organizational capacity of the foreign policy sector, are important features which suggest that it is inappropriate to project the conventional large-state oriented model of decision-making on the foreign policy behavior of microstates. This argument can be sustained by an examination of the more important features of the microstate foreign policy-making process.

Our point of departure is to suggest that microstate foreign policy decision-making is predominantly an individual rather than a group process. Unlike the situation which prevails in larger political systems, the chief decision maker in the microstate is involved not merely in giving a final and formal assent to proposals submitted to him but he participates actively in the process of lower-level discussion of contextuating factors, and he may be centrally involved in the implementation of the decision as well. Singham (1967: 323) has claimed that the political processes of very small communities are characterized by a highly personalized form of government and an authoritarian form of decision-making. This pattern, however, is more likely to be found in new states, and is probably the outcome of their colonial experience. In situations of personal government one individual is predominantly influential in enunciating the goals of government, and often assumes complete responsibility for the execution of these goals as well. Such a situation can be contrasted with one of representative government in which the enunciation and execution of goals is basically the result of a process of interaction between cooperating and competing elites.

Some insights into the relative advantages and disadvantages of this type of decision process can be found in the contributions which have been made by researchers on group processes. Collins and Guetzkow (1964: 52-53) suggest that there are a number of factors which differentiate the productivity of an individual working alone from the productivity of the same individual working in a face-to-face decision-making group. They suggest that the group will have access to more extensive resources than an individual member, and that, depending on the nature of the task and the effectiveness of the group's interpersonal relations, these extra resources will either inhibit productivity or be used to produce an "assembly effect" bonus. What is a crucial feature is the extent to which the task lends itself to a division of labor. A task so structured that divisions of labor are impossible makes it difficult for the group to utilize its potentially superior resources.

Studies of group-decision processes (Collins and Guetzkow, 1964: 52-53) suggest, also, that the outputs of group effort will frequently be superior to that of an individual, because the pooling of individual judgments eliminates random error. The greater potential resources of a collection of individuals may mean, also, that the group is more likely to discover alternative solutions than a single individual. However, in the selective process of group deliberation, no consideration can be given to all alternatives and even then, there is likely to be a greater consumption of man-hours by the group than by an individual working alone. It should be noted, however, that while the direction of the available studies is to indicate that group members may achieve collectively more than the most superior members could achieve alone, the evidence is not method-ologically sophisticated enough to verify the specific mechanisms through which this comes about.

The situation in microstate decision-making of a process of policy formulation predominantly centered on a single individual can be contrasted with that which is usually found in larger states where policy-making is much more evidently the result of group efforts. Where foreign policy decisions are the outcomes of group processes it is rather difficult to establish the role played by particular individuals. However, in very small states decisions on foreign policy are usually made by the head of government, even where the formal role of foreign minister is performed by a different individual. In many microstates the Prime Minister is also the Minister of Foreign Affairs.[4] This combination of functions is unusual in larger states. As one writer (Frankel, 1963: 22) has suggested, the burdens of the foreign office, especially attendance at prolonged international conferences, render this combination of offices unworkable for any length of time.

As we have noted in the section in which the implications of very small size were discussed, the governments of microstates find it imperative to employ various methods of containing the costs of administrative overheads. One method frequently employed to reduce the costs of administration is to keep the number of ministers and their staffs to a workable minimum. Where it is impossible because of the nature of task differentiation to establish separate ministries, it is usual to find one minister presiding over them. In a situation of performance of multiple roles it is possible for different roles to compete for the attention of the decision maker, with the probable outcome of some degree of neglect of one of them. Because foreign policy demands may not appear to be as pressing as domestic ones primacy may be given to domestic considerations. Alternatively the decision maker may have a strong orientation toward the external environment, with its attraction of playing to a larger audience. The problem of multiple competences of major decision makers is that the reassessment of priorities to be attributed to different areas of policy is less likely to be made where there is little differentiation of competences and there is an absence of the debate characteristic of organizations in which there are a number of influential officials, each of whom can be entrusted with responsibility for a specific area of policy.

Kelman (1970) has noted that discussion about the importance of individual decision makers in the foreign policy-making process often centers on questions of whether the decision maker is an antonomous agent or whether his behavior can be shown to be subject to powerful constraint. However, he suggests (1970: 5) that while it can be taken for granted that foreign policy decision makers operate in a highly constrained environment the important question is what kinds of constraints operate under what circumstances. The extent to which the various constraints come into play may depend on the occasion for decision, and on numerous other factors. In the complex interrelationship of the variables which are present in the decision-making process, structural factors may create dispositional constraints, and dispositional factors may create structural constraints. If we accept this proposition, we may argue that in microstate decision processes the peculiar outward orientation of policy may be attributed to perceived limitations of domestic capabilities, and, the need to depend on external support to achieve domestic objectives. In such a situation, external constraints may be relatively more potent than domestic ones.

A number of writers (Benedict, 1967; Kroll, 1967) have drawn attention to the impact of very small size on the capability of the bureaucratic structures of microstates. This essentially is a problem of lack of critical mass. Because of the small size of the social structure, the most capable individuals may perceive domestic career opportunities to be limited and look for alternative satisfactions abroad. In very small societies, also, the narrow social parameters give rise to a high intensity of face-to-face interaction. This may accentuate both cooperative and conflictual relationships among individuals. While increased cooperation may enhance the making of decisions, the danger of increased intensity and occurrence of conflict is a factor likely to detract from the quality of the decisions which are made. In situations of high face-to-face interaction the possibility exists that advice which is tendered may be accepted, not on its objective merits, but, on the basis of evaluations of the worth of the person from whom it comes. There is also the danger that able individuals may be left permanently outside the decision process.

The bureaucracy is also likely to be short of experience in dealing with matters of foreign affairs in the new microstates. This is because the pattern of transfer of power employed by the former metropole usually involves the retention of control over the territory's foreign relations even after its capacity for internal self-government has been conceded. Even at that stage of devolution the very top of the decision- and policy-making pyramid often consists of foreign officials. Its removal, on independence, can loosen the whole substructure of political and bureaucratic leadership. In this state of immediate post-independence administrative fluidity, it is often difficult to find persons capable and willing to undertake positions of administrative responsibility. While one might regard inexperience of personnel as a temporary condition, the previously noted limited career opportunities in a very small administration make it extremely difficult for microstates to retain highly skilled officials. The tendency of these factors is to provide supports rather than to impose constraints on the freedom of the political leadership. Where political mobilization is based on a charismatic tradition there will be little emphasis on accountability to the mass public for policy choices. Political parties, parliaments, and public opinion will also tend to play a minimal role in the formation of policy.

In looking at foreign policy decision-making in microstates it is important to distinguish between the formal structure of the institutions which circumscribe the process, and the process as it operates. Many of the very small states of the contemporary international system have passed through a period of colonial tutelage. As Lee (1967) has noted, during the colonial period the metropolitan power has frequently established faithful replicas of her political institutions. Those microstates which have been British colonies have inherited institutions which have been patterned on the Westminister/Whitehall model. However, these institutions often do not perform similar functions to their counterparts in large states because of the peculiar social dynamics of small-scale societies. Small scale appears to enforce a pattern of social compression. There seems to be a tendency toward convergence of the elite structures in the economic, political, and social systems of small-scale societies. Role relationships tend to be diffuse rather than functionally specific. Traditional patterns of diffusion of roles will hamper the operation of institutions which emphasize the performance of specific roles by their members.

Oxaal (1967: 142) has demonstrated that the traditional recruitment process to political organizations in very small states can be highly informal. Such a process of recruitment often stresses personal acquaintance and character endorsement by those already in the group. This means, in effect, that the attainment and maintenance of leadership positions proceed along a network of personal relationships. Loyalty to the leadership and conformity within the structure is given a greater emphasis than competitiveness and innovation. These factors are sources of support for the predominant role of the leader in the microstate decision-making process.

In decision-making analyses, an important point of focus is the role played by communication and information (Deutsch, 1963). Vital (1967: 22) has taken particular note of the disadvantages which their limited information and communication networks impose on the foreign policy-making machinery of small states. It is the contention of the present writer that this problem is found in a more accentuated form in microstates. We have noted earlier that the cost of government in very small states is proportionately higher than in larger states. Private sector limitations tend to require the public sector in microstates to become involved in a wide range of domestic activity. As a result, microstates will be able to devote only a very small proportion of their already limited resources to the conduct of international affairs. East (1973) has pointed out that in small states, resource limitations will be reflected in the size and the organization of the foreign affairs establishment. In microstates there are even greater limitations on the number of persons involved in the monitoring of international events and occurrences and in the execution of foreign-policy. Indeed, within the structure of the foreign affairs establishment the constraint of very small size precludes the conduct of important areas of activity. Since the establishment will be unable to cope with the entire range of international phenomena, the foreign ministry will usually place emphasis on a limited number of functional and geographic areas. In particular, the economic vulnerability of the state will direct the emphasis to economic issues.

Even where the scope of international involvement is consciously limited to a narrow range of issues, the resource deficiencies of the foreign affairs establishment will still impose significant disabilities. The foreign ministry may be unable to conduct the necessary research which should provide the basis for important foreign policy decisions. Within the foreign ministry manpower shortages may preclude the establishment of a separate research unit, and as a result it will be difficult to prepare adequate background papers. Often, background papers will have to be prepared by the same persons who are involved in the day-to-day problems of foreign policy and who are likely to place their emphasis on short-term considerations.

The difficulties which are encountered by the foreign establishment at its headquarters are likely to be paralleled in more acute fashion by its missions abroad. These missions will be located in the few capitals which the decision makers deem to be of vital importance to the promotion of their interests. Often, the external representation of microstates is restricted to two or three major capitals of the world. Microstates also attach importance to a presence at the United Nations headquarters, as well as at centers which provide the location for regional organizations. A great part of their activity will involve participation in international and regional conferences. The preference of small states for multilateral over traditional bilateral patterns of diplomatic exchange can be seen as an attempt to use low cost methods of interaction. (East, 1973). Deficiencies in its own machinery for collecting and processing of information will lead the very small state to rely heavily on information collected by international organizations and friendly states. The need to rely on others for information is likely to affect adversely the capacity of microstates to react to external events which may have important consequences for their vital interests. Because of their difficulty in interpreting the information which comes from the external environment, microstates will be slow to perceive various opportunities and constraints. Their foreign policy will tend to be reactions to phenomena emanating from the external environment, rather than a conscious process of attempting to achieve their objectives by positive externally directed actions.

The cumulative effect of the impact of very small size on microstate foreign policy decision-making is to reduce the resources which can be brought to bear on the formulation and execution of programmes of action. Shortages of financial and manpower resources would seem to direct decision makers to give priority to a few areas of major concern in foreign policy formulation. Even where such policies are carefully formulated, there are many factors outside the domestic environment which have important consequences for their outcomes. To understand the reasons for success or failure of such undertakings one must have a clear picture of the nature of the external environment in which they unfold. This environment is usually described as the international system. In the following section we shall examine its relevance to the foreign policy behavior of microstates.

MICROSTATES AND THE INTERNATIONAL SYSTEM

The international system approach provides a major theoretical perspective for the analysis of international behavior. Morton Kaplan

(1957) has provided the seminal study of relationships between and among the major actors in international politics. Kaplan has argued explicitly (1957: 60-74) that the type of international system is a major variable which accounts for differences in international behavior. For the purpose of analysis, Kaplan delineated six international systems and demonstrated how their characteristics affected the scope of the activities of various types of national actors. Other writers who have used the concept of system as a framework for analysis (Burton, 1968; McClelland, 1966; Modelski 1962) have not concentrated on types of international systems to the same degree, but have been concerned with the study of various types of behavior involving nation-states and other types of transnational actors. It can be stated, however, that the unifying theme which distinguishes studies utilizing the international systemic perspective from those based on other approaches is that relationships between major centers of activity in the international community are major variables which account for international political behavior. Although variations in emphasis can be detected, users of the international systems perspective generally define a system as a group of actors standing in characteristic relationships to each other, interacting on the basis of recognizable patterns, and subject to various contextual limitations (Young, 1968: 6).[5]

International system analysis focuses on interaction. The fact that human aggregates are the component units of international systems has tended to give rise to controversy between concrete and analytic definitions of international systems. The argument for definition of international systems in concrete terms has been put forward by Stanley Hoffmann (1965: 768) who advocated the analysis of such attributes of the system as its temporal and spatial limits, and the relationship between the system and its component units. Hoffmann's approach demonstrates that concrete constructs focus on the physical components of the phenomena under analysis (Young, 1968: 21) and, thus, require a historical treatment of actual events and situations.

The analytic approach to the definition of international systems emphasizes more abstract and heuristic qualities of the component phenomena. From this point of view, the international system can be regarded as composed of the interaction of various patterns of behavior expressed by the states in the process of conducting their foreign policies. The major differences between concrete and analytic definitions of international systems have been summarized by Young (1968: 22). He notes that while concrete constructs emphasize the component actors of international systems and tend to minimize the problems of empirical identification, they are apt to underline the unique qualities of specific systems. Analytical constructs focus on the aspects of international systems such as structures, processes, context, and the analytical aspects of actors such as number and type.

A number of scholars have argued that international behavior may be more effectively analyzed from the systemic perspective by focusing on interaction which takes place in environments less comprehensive than the global system. They have chosen, therefore, to concentrate their efforts on the study of international subsystems, subordinate systems, or regions (Banks, 1969; Bowman, 1968; Brecher, 1963; Cantori and Spiegel, 1969). In these studies, subordinate systems are identified according to six defining characteristics. These are:

(1) A delimited scope with primary stress on geographic region;
(2) the existence of at least three actors;
(3) that the actors, taken together, be distinctively recognized by other actors as constituting a specific community, region, or segment of the global system;
(4) that the members identify themselves as such;
(5) a relative inferiority of the units of power in the subordinate system to units in the dominant system; and
(6) that changes in the dominant system have a greater effect on the subordinate system than the reverse.

The proponents of the subordinate system concept have claimed that it is not possible to comprehend the operation of the international system unless inquiry also proceeds at the subsystemic level. They have pointed out that states operate at different levels and usually have various associations. Apart from being members of the global system they may also be members of more limited systems. Since different actions and decisions derive from different associations, it is useful to separate and correlate policy acts with specific membership roles. What seems to be needed, therefore, is a model which treats the actions performed by states in the global system or subsystem as expressions of their membership roles.

A recent attempt to relate the foreign policy actions to the performance by states of particular roles in the international system or subordinate systems has been made by Holsti (1970) by introducing the notion of national role conceptions. While recognizing the difficulty of transposing concepts used in intranational social analysis to the less formal and organized international setting, Holsti still suggests that the concept may generate significant insights into patterns of external behavior. Holsti

(1970: 242) suggests that the notion of "status" as that term has come to be used in analyses of international stratification, could be employed as an alternative to the behavioral referent usually denoted as "position" in sociological role analysis. In support of his argument Holsti cites the usage of classifications of states in terms of superpowers, middle powers, and so on, as tentative indicators of their international status. While he admits that whether or not these distinctions are crucial in the minds of policy makers may be difficult to test, he claims, nevertheless, that it is reasonable to assume that those responsible for making decisions and taking actions for the state are aware of international status distinctions and that their policies reflect this awareness.

Holsti defines a national role conception to include the policy maker's own definitions of the general kinds of decisions, commitments, rules, and actions suitable to their state, and of the functions, if any, their state should perform on a continuing basis in the international system or in the subordinate international system. He suggests that to explain different national role conceptions in different states one might look at a wide variety of sources. Among these he includes location and major topographical features; national, economic and technical resources; traditional policies; socioeconomic demands and needs as expressed through different strata of the domestic polity; national values, ideologies, etc., mood of public opinion, and the personality or political needs of key policy makers. Holsti notes, also, that national role conceptions are related to, or buttressed by, the role prescriptions coming from the external environment. He regards the sources of such prescriptions as including the structure of the international system; system-wide values; general legal principles which ostensibly command universal support; the rules, traditions, and expectations of states as expressed in charters on international and regional organizations, "world opinion," multilateral and bilateral treaties; and, less formal or implicit commitments and "understandings."

It seems reasonable to argue that the extent to which the features of the international system exert an impact on the choice of foreign policy undertakings of states will depend on the perceptions of the extent to which they impose constraints or provide opportunities for the undertakings which are embraced by the decision makers. At the same time, the extent to which they exert an impact on the outcome of these undertakings will depend on the extent to which the perceptions of the decision makers were congruent with reality. These hypotheses can be clarified by a number of supplementary ones. Firstly, where the decision maker considers his action to be in his state's vital national interest, and in particular where this is defined in exclusive terms, external prescriptions will not play a major role. Secondly, where the decision maker perceives that his undertaking can be carried out without need for external support, external prescriptions will not be a major determinant. The hypothesis which can be adduced about the microstate is that while its lack of domestic capabilities will give it a general orientation to seek external support in attaining its objectives, information and communication will play a vital part in the process by which external factors become salient.

The study of national role conceptions provides a basis for relating international systemic phenomena to the foreign policy actions of states. National role conceptions can, thus, be regarded as intervening variables linking the arrangement of relations between and among the major centers of activity in the global community and a state's foreign policy actions. We have noted in our discussion of decision-making, that the explanation of choices of certain courses of action by policy makers must be framed in terms of processes occurring within the actor's psychological environment. The central premise of the model which links national role conceptions, foreign policy actions, and international systemic relationships, is that in articulating national roles, foreign policy decision makers formulate their actions on the basis of constraints and opportunities which they perceive to exist in the external environment.

There would seem to be some merit in collecting data which would indicate the national role conceptions held by microstates. Holsti has claimed that his investigations of the official statements of the representatives of certain types of states, particularly the small states of Latin America, suggested that national role conceptions were not significant aspects of their foreign policy. He regarded this discovery as an indication that the governments of those states have no foreign policy in the sense of a coherent set of objectives guiding day-to-day diplomatic action. Holsti claimed that, except for commercial matters, states which articulated few role conceptions do not appear to try to change external conditions in their favor and they see no continuing external tasks for themselves, although their internal life is highly vulnerable to disturbances coming from the external environment. As a result, he came to the conclusion that such states are objects rather than actors in international relationships.

It is not surprising to find that states which participate to a limited extent in international affairs and which restrict their participation to a few issues articulate few national role conceptions. This finding accords with the conventional assumption of a status quo orientation by small states and the avoidance of behavior which will alienate more powerful states. This behavioral pattern will be even more noticeable in the policies of microstates. The leaders of microstates will tend to avoid engaging in ambiguous external behavior so as to preclude the possibility of their actions being interpreted as aggressive.

The concept of national roles can be used not only to focus on the issue of the kinds of foreign policy actions which are associated with specific national roles, but also on the effect which the playing of various roles has on system stability and change. To perform the latter type of analysis, one must look at the structure of the internal system. The contemporary international system contains many different types of actors. In the traditional literature distinctions have been made between states, which represent one of the major types of actors, on the basis of their relative capabilities. A well-known distinction classifies states as superpowers, great powers, middle powers, and small powers. Microstates can be added as the bottom of this continuum of size. What is to be noted is that classifications which rank states in terms of their relative capabilities suggest, in effect, that there is a stratification system in world society. A stratification system consists of hierarchy of unequal positions. The implication, therefore, of an international stratification system as an analytical construct is that the position of a state in the hierarchy of world society has important consequences for its international behavior. Lagos (1963) has studied the effect of the pattern of stratification in the contemporary international system on the behavior of underdeveloped nations. In a more recent work, East (1969) has looked at the consequences of stratification for the international system itself.

The use of an international systems perspective allows both an analysis of the effect of the existence of different classes of states on the functioning of the international system as well as an investigation of the consequences of status differences for the foreign policies of particular classes of states. Our concern with the implications of very small size for patterns of foreign policy behavior makes it imperative that we examine the hypotheses which can be derived from both points of view. Dealing first with the possible impact of different classes of states on the functioning of the international system, we can take note of the typology that Keohane (1969) has suggested. He distinguishes between system-determining states which play a critical role in shaping the system; system-influencing states, which cannot expect individually to dominate a system but may, nevertheless, be able significantly to influence its nature through unilateral as well as multilateral actions; system-affecting states which can only exert a significant impact on the system by working through small groups or alliances, or through universal or regional organizationa; and system-ineffectual states, which can do little to influence the system-wide forces that affect them, except in groups so large that each state has minimal influence, and which may themselves be dominated by larger powers. Keohane (1969: 295-6), in effect, equates this classification with the traditional one which distinguishes between superpowers, great powers, middle powers, and small states. His approach is rather deterministic and it is not surprising that he comes to the conclusion that the foreign policy of system-ineffectual states is an adjustment to reality and not a rearrangement of it.

Whether small states are system-ineffectual even at the level of the global system is debatable. Claude (1969: 54) has suggested that states may contribute to international instability not only by active policies but also by passive provocation. Claude suggests that a state may be so weak, so deficient in economic viability, and so lacking in social cohesion and political stability that it represents a kind of a vacuum, virtually inviting the competitive intrusion of outside powers. Claude's comment serves to direct our focus to the fact that the "viability" of very small states may be more dependent on the existence of systemic phenomena than on any capabilities which are directly possessed by them. In fact, the emergence to political independence of very small, weak states with fragile economic and political systems, which would have been inconceivable in an earlier historical period, is in itself the result of system-wide forces, such as the recognition of self-determination as an international value.

An alternative point of view about the systemic role of small states has been suggested by Vellut (1967) who draws attention to the fact that there was a general acceptance of the notion that the existence of a multiplicity of very small states in Europe in an earlier historical epoch was essential for the maintenance of the peace. Because of their limited capacity to engage in violent international activity the notion of the contribution of very small states to the maintenance of peace still lingers on. The true facts of the matter may well be that microstates may be able to make little impact on the global system. On the other hand, their role may be considerable in more narrowly delimited regional arenas.

Our concern with the analysis of the foreign policies of microstates leads us to consider a number of ways in which the structure of the international system may influence their international behavior. As a point of departure it must be stressed that while the perception of constraints or opportunities in the external environment will act as a central determinant of the decision makers' actions, whether those features do exist will determine their success. Our major hypothesis is that microstates are likely to be highly dependent on systemic factors for support for their undertakings, in view of their limited domestic resources. It can be suggested also that since the activities of microstates are likely to comprise a very small part of the total transactions in the international system they may be successful in those transactions even when they infringe upon system rules. In the context of the global system, the interests of microstates will appear to be low-keyed and they are less likely to meet with resistance in promoting them than would be the case with larger states.

From the international systems perspective it is useful to consider how the low status of microstates is likely to affect their participation in world affairs. We noted in our discussion of the limitations of the microstate foreign policy establishment that deficiencies in money and manpower will restrict the scope of its participation in world affairs. The degree of participation in the international system can be related, also, to the interests of microstates. It is evident that those actors in the international system which hold high positions will participate most in its affairs. Since the interests of such states will suffer the greatest damage in the event that there is a drastic change they will participate extensively in the affairs of the system in order to maintain the status quo. One can also conceive of a situation in which other large states, which have adequate resources, would participate to a large degree in the attempt to change the system. East (1969) has carried out an empirical investigation which confirms that participation in the affairs of the international system as the continuum of states proceeds downwards from those states which rank high to those which are low.

Participation in world affairs can be looked at, not only in terms of its magnitude, but also in terms of its geographical scope. We have noted that useful distinctions may be made between the global, regional, and contiguous arenas of international activity. The substantive content of participation can also be differentiated in terms of whether it refers to issues which are economic, military/strategic, or political/diplomatic.[6] The major hypothesis that can be made about microstate participation in international affairs is that participation will be based predominantly on economic issues. A supplementary hypothesis which can be made is that participation will be concentrated at two levels: the global system and the contiguous arena. In promoting their political survival, as well as their economic welfare interests, microstates will tend to engage in activity at the broad, international system level. Recognition that their viability is conditional will encourage such states to engage in patterns of foreign policy interaction which emphasize a diversified pattern of dependence on the system as a whole as the alternative to dependence on one or a few states. Thus, in their search for economic assistance microstates tend to look to the multilateral agencies and the United Nations as a counterweight to dependence on bilateral arrangements. Further, even though theirs will be a client status, participation in the activities of such agencies will provide microstates with a degree of involvement which they may regard as an acceptable return for the commitment of their limited resources.

The emphasis likely to be placed by microstates on the contiguous arena as a salient environment of their foreign policies can be attributed to such factors as the need to be in a position to respond to phenomena which are nearer at hand, and thus more likely to have an intrusive impact on their domestic systems as well as the possibility of producing desired effects with their limited capabilities. However, such dangers and possibilities will depend on the relative degrees of similarity or discrepancy in the capabilities of the microstate and those of the other member states of its contiguous environment. In concluding the discussion of the relevance of the international systems perspective to the understanding of microstate foreign policies, it is useful to emphasize that our particular concern requires that we adopt a perspective in which attention is directed to the discovery of the extent to which the system imposes constraints, or, alternatively, provides opportunities and supports for microstate external activity. Our fundamental task is to attempt to understand patterns of relationships which cut across national boundaries. The use of the systemic perspective allows the analyst to move from a relatively unstructured notion of the external environment to one in which phenomena are identified at various systemic strata. Thus, one may attempt to trace the possible impact of a foreign policy undertaking as it moves from more immediate to wider international contexts. Such a theoretical approach will assist in the prediction of possible outcomes and provide a basis for determining the effectiveness of foreign policy. However, as Hanrieder (1965: 109) has pointed out, to achieve a useful working measure of effectiveness, one must be able to understand not only internal organizational factors and influences on decisions, and the external constraints or supports for the resulting actions, but the interrelationship of these different levels. In the following section this interrelationship will be discussed.

SIZE AND INTERNAL-EXTERNAL INTERDEPENDENCIES

In the preceding sections of this paper we have examined the impact of domestic and external factors on the international behavior of microstates. It is important to recognize that each of these approaches to analysis can provide only partial explanations of international behavior. A study of domestic factors can highlight organizational variables which serve to explain the process by which objectives are conceived and defined. Conversely, by focusing on the external environment it is possible to identify factors which enhance or limit the objectives chosen by the decision makers. Success or failure of particular actions can often be explained in terms of the accuracy with which decision makers perceive such external factors. Despite the recognition that foreign policy is a dynamic process of interaction involving both domestic and external factors no satisfactory method has yet been devised for integrating the two perspectives into a single framework. The major difficulty stems from the differences in the levels and units of analysis of the two conceptual approaches (Singer, 1961). Different sets of assumptions must be employed to explain and predict behavior at different levels of organization such as decision-making groups, nation-states, or international systems (Brody, 1969: 114).

Some scholars have been particularly concerned with the analysis of the interdependence between national actors and their external environments (Hanrieder, 1965; Rosenau, 1969: 44-63). They have held that actor objectives can be understood only by a simultaneous focus on the domestic and the external environments (Hanrieder, 1965: 118). Rosenau has stated categorically that in order to understand the dynamic process of international behavior it is necessary to develop propositions linking the functioning of the actor to its external environment and relating changes in its behavior to variations in its environment (1967b: 985). Rosenau contends that such relationships can be explained by the concept of "linkage" which he defines (1969: 45) as a recurrent sequence of behavior that originates in one system and is reacted to in another.

The major problem presented by Rosenau's framework for the analysis of linkages is that it suggests a very large number of variables which may be relevant to the understanding of foreign policy actions and their outcomes without offering any method for determining their relative importance. However, the linkage concept suggests a number of relationships between the size of a state and its internal-external interdependencies which are worth investigating. The most important of these relationships is that of external dependence in the functioning of the domestic system. Rosenau defines this condition as "penetration" (1966: 65). For Rosenau, a national political system is penetrated when that system embraces actors who are not formally members of it, but who nevertheless not only exert influence on it but participate in its political processes as well. He claims that penetrated systems are characterized by a shortage of capabilities which provides legitimacy for the participation of nonmembers in their politics (1966: 68).

In our analysis of microstates, there seems to be a direct relationship between the size of a state and the extent to which it is penetrated. A great deal of emphasis has been placed on the relationship between very small size and deficiencies in domestic resources. A consideration of the phenomenon of penetration suggests that the shortage of capabilities will make microstates relatively more likely to be penetrated than larger states. Further, the small scale of their societies will make penetration a relatively more pervasive process. Penetration can be distinguished in terms of the issue-areas in which it takes place. We have noted that in small-scale societies there is often a scarcity of capital for investment and an absence of private entrepreneurs. Very small countries tend to be relatively more dependent on outsiders for the supply of skills and investment than larger states. Because of the pressures on the budgetary resources of their governments, very small states tend to be heavily dependent on foreign aid, particularly for infrastructural projects. In the contemporary international system a large proportion of the international economic transactions which are carried on are undertaken by multinational corporations. It seems that an external strategy which can be adopted by very small states would be to cultivate diplomatic support to counterbalance the potential pressures which can be brought on their freedom of action by foreign private interests.

Another interesting relationship is that of an observable tendency of states to imitate the behavior of others. The behavior of microstates is particularly prone to this type of dependence. In our earlier discussion of the decision-making process in very small states we identified certain deficiencies in organizational structure, and in systems of information and communication. The activity of elite groups in very small societies tends to be imitative of that of similar groups in larger societies abroad. Such imitative behavior is often reinforced by patterns of institutional reiteration.

The study of external-internal interdependencies in foreign policy behavior can be facilitated by an analysis of the referents used by actors in the process of conceiving of and defining their objectives. Hanrieder (1965: 118; 1967: 980) has suggested that such referents are of three types: the internal, the external, and the systemic. Objectives defined on the basis of internal referents do not require reference to phenomena outside of the state. Behavior deriving from external referents is dependent for its realization on the behavior of other members of the international system. Systemic referents on the other hand are factors such as the existing patterns of power and purpose in the international system, the perception of which stimulates the choice of objectives by the decision maker (Hanrieder, 1967: 980).

There seems to be strong support for the argument that microstate objectives will be determined more by external and systemic referents than by internal referents. Indeed, it can be argued that not only are their domestic objectives likely to be determined by a process of comparison with other states, but that such objectives cannot be attained without involvement in external activity.

It seems reasonable to argue that the size of a state is a critical factor which determines the pattern of the relationships between its domestic system and the external environment. Domestic capability limitations predispose microstates to be highly dependent on the external environment. Such dependence will restrict the range and scope of their foreign policy actions. The participation of nonmembers in the process of decision-making can limit the capacity of the state to formulate policies which are fully expressive of the national interest. Where such policies are conceived implementation may be made difficult because the necessary resources are controlled by foreigners.

The key factors linking phenomena in the domestic and external environments to the foreign policy behavior of microstates are the perceptions and orientations of the decision makers. Their view of the possibility for effective action in dealing with domestic issues can be crucial in determining their participation in external affairs. It is possible that success at the domestic level may give a sense of confidence and encourage them to focus on foreign issues. However, failure to cope effectively may be blamed on "foreign devils." The corollary of such an approach can be an almost total concentration on phenomena which originate abroad.

TOWARD VALIDATION OF HYPOTHESES ABOUT MICROSTATES

In the introductory section of this paper we noted that we were concerned mainly with the problem of definition and classification of microstates. We stressed, therefore, that our major hypothesis that very small size is a key independent variable in accounting for patterns of foreign policy behavior should be capable of being tested empirically. For this reason we defined foreign policy behavior as the discrete acts of recognizable national authorities. This section of the paper will discuss an approach to the collection of data which could be used to test our hypotheses.

The empirical analysis of patterns of international behavior of a particular class of states requires an exhaustive collection of data which can be manipulated to differentiate the characteristic acts of that class of states from those which are characteristic of other classes of states. The compilation of a series of data which is descriptive of the foreign policy actions of all the states which are members of the contemporary international system would be a formidable task for the individual researcher. Fortunately, there exist a number of data collections which can be used for comparative research. These collections are based on the concept of "events/interaction analysis."

Pioneering work has been done by Charles McClelland (1969: 711-24) to develop a series of ad hoc categories to classify all discrete foreign policy events which have been reported in public sources. McClelland has compiled the World Event/Interaction Survey (WEIS) which classifies foreign policy behavior into twenty-two ad hoc categories. The data collection consists of the international events reported in the daily issues of the New York *Times* from January 1966 to the present. Since then, other collections have been initiated using alternative sources of data. One of these, the project on Comparative Research on the Events of Nations (Project CREON), is a compilation of events which were initiated by thirty-four nation states during randomly selected quarters of each of the years in the decade 1959-1968. The source of the information for the events recorded by Project CREON is *Deadline Data on World Affairs*. This source differs from reports carried in newspapers in that it is partly processed, since it attempts to provide data required by researchers, rather than information for the interest of the general reader. Project CREON is of particular interest to the concerns of this paper in that its ad hoc categories of acts have been formulated so as to distinguish features of behavior, such as its verbal or nonverbal dimensions, and the instruments which are used. Indeed, the scheme has been framed to provide specific answers to questions of the relationship between the size of the originating state and the type, frequency, and the intensity of its foreign policy behavior.

As we have noted, the organizing concept behind the data collections is that of the event. An event is generally defined as official acts between states. Azar et al. (1972: 61) regard an event as "any overt input or output of the type 'who does what to or with whom and when' which may have ramifications for the behavior of an international actor or actors." For this definition to be operational the event must be recorded at least once in any publicly available source that meets certain specified requirements. Azar et al. (1972: 62) maintain that an event has five components: actor, target, activity, issue-area, and time, and that all these components must exist within the source if an event is to be identified.

Although events data analysis has attempted to establish explicit operational definitions of behavior, data collected on foreign policy events can depend on the subjective interpretations of those who code the data. For this reason, considerable attention has been devoted to the development of coding rules (Hermann, 1971: 295-321) and the improvement of reliability in the coding of events by different coders (Taylor and Hudson, 1972: 391-423). Such reliability is important since events must be capable of being allocated to a limited number of mutually exclusive types. It is on the basis of such a classification that differences between states can be identified.

An approach which begins with an explicit conception and operational definition of foreign policy activity is essential if meaningful empirical research is to be conducted on the foreign policy behavior of microstates. The emphasis on public reports of foreign policy behavior as the raw information on which the analysis should be based is an important factor in support of the use of an events/interaction focus. However, as Scolnick (1972) has pointed out in a recent critique, the events data approach introduces problems as well as possibilities. A major difficulty derives from the necessity to use newspaper sources which often have biases in the coverage of events, as well as differing editorial conceptions about what is newsworthy. More importantly, the principal advantage of the events data approach would be to permit the conduct of analysis which is cumulative with that of other scholars and could add to the current stock of empirically derived generalizations about foreign policy behavior.

A serious problem which may face events based research on the external behavior of microstates is that of information. Useful analysis can be carried out only if there is a sufficient number of events recorded. Reporting sources which provide a global coverage of events are unlikely to record many events which involve microstates because their publishers may not consider such occurrences to be newsworthy unless the circumstances are unusual. Microstate activities may receive a greater degree of coverage in regional sources but there may be serious practical difficulties in obtaining data on microstates from regions with no single authoritative agency which reports foreign policy events. Ultimately, one may have to rely on national papers published in the microstates for a source of events data. This, however, can be expected to raise the difficulty of comparison of frequencies of occurrence of events as reported in different national newspapers. Indeed, there is likely to be differential coverage if the press in some microstates is relatively more active and effective in gleaning news of foreign policy activity than in others.

The empirical analysis of microstate foreign policy activity in terms of the events data approach is also likely to be faced with numerous other problems. Among these, one can include the problem that the events data approach has been developed out of an interest by researchers in the study of conflict, and of crisis situations. If the conventional assumption that microstates will be engaged in few crisis situations, because of a recognized need to defer to the wishes of larger states, is valid, then, the crisis perspective is inappropriate to the study of microstate foreign policy behavior. In order to map the pattern of exchanges between microstates and other members of the contemporary international system, it may be necessary to operationalize the concept of an event in a way which will be able to take account of the more routine activities which are likely to characterize microstate international behavior. While these are practical problems, it is to be hoped that they can be surmounted since cumulative empirical research is an essential technique for extending our knowledge of foreign policy behavior.

The deficiencies of an events data approach to the study of microstate foreign policy behavior can be offset by collecting other types of data which are indicative of microstate patterns of interaction. Data on the frequency and the number of exchanges with their external environment such as flows of mail and other communications, trade, and movements of human individuals, may assist in establishing a profile of microstate transactions. Comparative data on the size of the foreign affairs establishment, in terms of personnel and budgetary commitments, will provide important indicators of foreign policy-making capacity. The number and size of diplomatic missions, and accreditations abroad as well as number of accreditations received by microstates, can be used as major indicators of international status, and participation in world affairs. Additional indicators of participation would be representation in international and regional organizations and attendance at regional and international conferences.

While aggregate information can be used to establish characteristic foreign policy profiles of microstates, the understanding of the operation of their decision-making processes will require detailed study of the attitudes, perceptions, and major value orientations of foreign policy decision makers and their advisers, as well as those of elites and influentials in micro-societies. This type of information could be obtained through the use of survey techniques. In view of the small number of persons who would have to be interviewed, the information could be obtained at a lower cost and more quickly than that which could be derived from similar investigations in larger states.

Empirical studies of foreign policy behavior necessary to validate hypotheses which are derived from a deductive process of analysis can be carried out at a lower cost in microstates than in larger states. Indeed, because of their small size, the researcher can achieve a sharper and more concise focus in a study of microstates than one dealing with larger states. This is because microstates have a more transparent social structure and key individuals can be more easily detected. Studies of communication flows are also made easier by their smaller communication network, although the researcher would have to direct his attention more to informal communications than to formal communications.

CONCLUSION

The basic working premise of our discussion is that the size of a state is the major factor which determines its behavior. Our basic argument has been that for analytical purposes, size should be treated as the independent variable and foreign policy behavior as the dependent variable. Our approach has been a deductive one in which we have examined the impact of very small size on the total capabilities of the state. The general direction of our argument has been that very small states have a relatively lower level of capabilities than larger states. Viewed against the totality of demands on their resources all modern states experience a scarcity of capabilities. Domestic constituency pressures impose on decision makers the necessity to give priority to the demands of the domestic environment. No leader who consistently turns away from such demands could seriously hope to have a long or peaceful tenure of office. The domestic environment, then, absorbs a high proportion of the state's total capabilities. The extent to which the state can participate in external affairs is determined essentially by the size of its surplus capabilities. In very small states, surplus capabilities are minimal.

The very low levels of surplus capabilities of microstates would suggest that their participation in international affairs will be greatly restricted. Viewed, however, in terms of its behavioral referents, the verbal and nonverbal aspects of participation in international affairs must be distinguished. Lacking the resources to engage in deeds, microstates participate by words. The content of such participation is frequently an attempt to augment their limited domestic resources by cooperative international action. Indeed, the need to depend on the external environment for support can impose on microstates a necessity to participate in international affairs to a much greater extent than larger states. The acceptance of assistance and support from one or a few donors can impose a reciprocal condition of dependence. Faced with the impossibility of avoiding dependence, the second best alternative for the microstate is to seek to balance its total dependence among a multiplicity of sources. In implementing that strategy the microstate can become highly involved in foreign policy activity.

Scarcity of manpower and material resources imposes on decision makers the requirement that they be highly selective in their foreign policy activity. Success in foreign policy is more likely to follow from a careful choice of a limited number of issues on which attention will be concentrated than from a diffuse foreign policy orientation. The possibility of success can be enhanced by concentrating on a single arena for the prosecution of the major issues of foreign policy. However, the prospects for the successful conduct of foreign policy undertakings by microstates are likely to be impeded by the problem of a low capacity for persistence. On the one hand microstates lack the resources which are required to support prolonged engagement in negotiation. On the other, the domestic style of decision-making and the multiple competencies of leaders may reinforce the tendency toward sporadic attention to foreign policy issues.

The foreign policy issues which stimulate the greatest amount of microstate concern are economic ones. On the successful prosecution of such issues their continued survival may well depend. However, the scope for the attainment of economic objectives through foreign policy activity may be considerable. Not only does the pursuit of improvements in economic welfare carry a high degree of international legitimacy, but it is also possible that where micro states infringe international principles in seeking to obtain such improvements they may meet with less resistance in view of the limited capacity of those infringements to have a destabilizing effect on the system. It should be noted also that the limited nature of their demands makes it possible for other states to assist microstates at no great expense of resources.

The deficiencies of their domestic resource base imposes on micro states the necessity to depend to a high degree on the external environment for support. The acceptance of assistance from abroad may restrict the capacity of decision makers to formulate and implement domestic programmes which are intended to improve the welfare of members of the national society at the expense of that of nonmembers.

Penetration may involve restrictions on the pursuit of other national interests. Faced with limited and difficult areas of choice there is a heavy burden placed on the leaders of microstates to evaluate and forecast the possible consequences of their action. However, while they have little margin for error, both lack of experience and the absence of machinery for research and analysis can restrict their capacity to perceive constraints and opportunities which exist in the external environment. Foreign policy may be excessive reactions to unanticipated events rather than an active process of promotion of domestic objectives.

The difficulties which microstates experience in conforming to the traditional model of state behavior should not be used as a basis for excluding them from scholarly analysis. The study of these miniscule communities may reveal important general features of international behavior which could be discovered only at greater costs in research on larger states. Indeed, microstate polities might be used as laboratories for the study of political processes in general. Microstate foreign policy processes could be regarded as a microcosm of the larger process of foreign policy formulation and execution. Such an approach will be possible if the researcher accepts the proposition that any political process can be regarded as a specific example of the operation of a larger and more general process of activity rather than a unique and incomparable arena of activity.

The rapid increase in the number of very small states in the contemporary international system can be regarded as an indication that despite the significant changes which have occurred in the techniques and instrumentalities of international interaction, historical notions still pervade the underlying philosophy of organization of world affairs. Traditional concepts of international behavior may fail to provide a satisfactory paradigm on which very small states can base their choices of appropriate courses of external behavior. Concepts of distance and physical discontinuity provide the underlying support for the legal cachet of "state." Yet both the dynamics and patterns of external behavior of microstates may differ little from those of other small communities, which despite their encapsulation in larger states still interact with the external environment. It seems, however, that while very small states may appear as curious anomalies in the contemporary world of international giants, in the absence of a satisfactory alternative they will continue to maintain a separate independence. It is this prospect which makes the study of their foreign policies a relevant endeavor by students of international affairs.

NOTES

1. The term "independent variables" is frequently used in formal theory building to refer to those factors in the particular theoretical formulation which account for the variance in the behavior under study. The behavior which undergoes this variation is termed the "dependent variable."

2. Taylor (1969) used cluster analysis in an attempt to separate microstates from "real" states. He applied this technique to 181 territories for which data on Gross National Product, population, and area were available, and standardized the values of each aggregate to weight each variable equally. He obtained clusters of states by separating those whose distances among themselves (measured in terms of the values of the three variables) were small as compared with their distances to other states. He discovered that the size of the cluster depended on the choice of cutoff point, but that there was no very obvious cutoff point between microstates and "real" states.

3. Relationships between variables can be measured by such statistical techniques as the construction of correlation matrices or the use of factor analysis. However, such techniques cannot by themselves indicate the precise nature of the relationship between the variables.

4. Modelski (1970: 139-140) presents a list of the world's foreign ministers in 1965. Eleven of the persons listed were foreign ministers of states which would fall within our classification of microstates. Of those eleven foreign ministers, five of them functioned concurrently as the Prime Minister.

5. It is impossible to present a concise summary of the large volume of literature which has been written on systems, or within the frame of reference of systems analysis. In political analysis the concept of system has been used to express the dynamic nature of activities which involve both formal and informal political processes and structures (Easton, 1963; Almond, 1965). In applying the system concept to political analysis scholars have tended to avoid the rigorous approach of general systems theory which requires that a variety of operations be carried out, preferably by several disciplines, to establish the existence of a specific system.

6. James Rosenau (1966: 73-74) has pointed out that in the foreign policy field there are numerous indications that the nature of the issue is crucial in determining how external behavior unfolds. He has argued, in consequence, that the boundaries of political systems ought to be drawn vertically in terms of "issue-areas" as well as horizontally in terms of geographic areas. Rosenau has borrowed the concept of "issue-areas" from Dahl (1961) who discovered in his research on community power that political systems differ according to the issue which is being processed.

REFERENCES

ALLISON, G. T. (1969) "Conceptual models and the Cuban missile crisis." Amer. Pol. Sci. Rev. 63, 3: 689-718.

ALMOND, G. A. (1965) "A developmental approach to political systems." World Politics 17, 1: 183-214.

AZAR, E. E, R. A. BRODY, and C. A. McCLELLAND (1972) International Events Interaction Analysis: Some Research Considerations. Sage Professional Papers in International Studies, 1, 02-001. Beverly Hills and London: Sage Pubns.

BANKS, M. (1969) "Systems analysis and the study of regions." International Studies Q. 13, 4: 335-360.

BENEDICT, B. [ed.] (1967) Problems of Smaller Territories. London: Athlone Press.

BRECHER, M. (1963) "International relations and Asian studies: the subordinate state system of Southern Asia." World Politics 15, 2: 213-235.

BOWMAN, L. (1968) "The subordinate state system of Southern Africa." International Studies Q. 12, 3: 231-261.

BRODY, R. A. (1969) "The study of international politics *qua* science." pp. 110-128 in K. Knorr and J. N. Rosenau (eds.) Contending Approaches to International Politics. New Jersey: Princeton Univ. Press.

BURGESS, P. M. (1970) "Nation-typing for foreign policy analysis: a partitioning procedure for constructing typologies." pp. 1-50 in E. H. Fedder (ed.) Methodological Concerns in International Studies. St. Louis: Univ. of Missouri Press.

BURTON, J. (1968) Systems, States, Diplomacy and Rules. London: Cambridge Univ. Press.

CANTORI, L. and S. SPIEGEL (1969) "International regions: a comparative approach to five subordinate systems." International Studies Q. 13, 4: 361-380.

CLAUDE, I. L. Jr. (1969) "Economic development, aid and international political stability." pp. 49-58 in R. W. Cox (ed.) International Organization: World Politics. London: Macmillan.

COLLINS, B. and H. GUETZKOW (1964) A Social Psychology for Group Decision Processes. New York: Wiley and Sons.

DAHL, R. (1961) Who Governs? New Haven: Yale Univ. Press.

DEUTSCH, K. (1963) The Nerves of Government. New York: Free Press.

EAST, M. A. (1973) "Size and foreign policy behavior: a test of two models." World Politics 25, 4: 556-576.

――― (1969) Stratification and International Politics: An Empirical Study Employing the International Systems Approach. Ph.D. Dissertation. New Jersey: Princeton Univ.

EASTON, D. (1963) The Political System. New Jersey: Prentice-Hall.

ETZIONI, A. (1968) The Active Society. New York: Free Press.

FRANKEL, J. (1963) The Making of Foreign Policy. London: Oxford Univ. Press.

HANRIEDER, W. (1967) "Compatibility and consensus: a proposal for the conceptual linkage of external and internal dimensions of foreign policy." Amer. Pol. Sci. Rev. 61, 4: 971-82.

――― (1965) "Actor objectives and international systems." Journal of Politics, 27, 1: 109-132.

HARRIS, W. L. (1970) "Microstates in the United Nations—a broader purpose." Columbia Journal of Transnational Law 9, 1: 23-53.

HERMANN, C. F. (1972) "Policy classification: a key to the comparative study of foreign policy." pp. 58-79 in J. N. Rosenau, V. Davis and M. A. East (eds.) The Analysis of International Politics. New York: Free Press.

――― (1971) "What is a foreign policy event?" pp. 295-321 in W. Hanrieder (ed.) Comparative Foreign Policy. New York: David McKay Co.

――― and M. A. EAST (1972) Do Nation Types Account for Foreign Policy Behavior? Washington: American Political Science Association. (mimeo)

HOFFMANN, S. (1965) The State of War: Essays on the Theory and Practice of International Politics. New York: Frederick A. Praeger.

HOLSTI, K. J. (1971) "Retreat from Utopia: international relations theory 1945-1970." Canadian Journal of Political Science 4, 2: 165-177.

––– (1970) "National role conceptions in the study of foreign policy." International Studies Q. 14, 3: 233-309.

JOHNSON, S. (1967) "Hierarchical clustering schemes." Psychometrika, 32, 3: 241-254.

KAPLAN, M. (1957) System and Process in International Politics. New York: Wiley and Sons.

KEGLEY, C. W. Jr. (1973) A General Empirical Typology of Foreign Policy Behavior. Sage Professional Papers in International Studies, 2, 02-014, Beverly Hills and London: Sage Pubns.

KELMAN, H. (1970) "The role of the individual in international relations: some conceptual and methodological considerations." Journal of International Affairs 24, 1: 1-17.

KEOHANE, R. (1969) "Lilliputian dilemmas: small states in international politics." International Organization 23, 2: 291-310.

KROLL, M. (1967) "Political leadership and administrative communications: the case study of Trinidad and Tobago." Social and Economic Studies, Jamaica 16, 1: 17-33.

LAGOS, G. (1963) International Stratification and Underdeveloped Countries. Chapel Hill: Univ. of North Carolina Press.

LEE, J. M. (1967) Colonial Policy and Good Government. Oxford: Clarendon Press.

LINDBLOM, C. (1959) "The science of muddling through." Public Administration Rev. 19, 79-88.

McCLELLAND, C. A. (1972) "Some effects of theory from the international event analysis movement," pp. 15-43 in International Events Interaction Analysis: Some Research Considerations, E. Azar, R. Brody, and C. McClelland. Sage Professional Paper in International Studies, 1, 02-001. Beverly Hills and London: Sage Pubns.

––– (1966) Theory and the International System. New York: Macmillan.

––– and G. HOGGARD (1969) "Conflict patterns in the interactions among nations," pp. 711-724 in J. N. Rosenau (ed.) International Politics and Foreign Policy, Revised Edition, New York: Free Press.

MODELSKI, G. (1970) "The world's foreign ministers: a political elite." J. of Conflict Resolution 15, 2: 135-176.

––– (1962) A Theory of Foreign Policy. London: Pall Mall Press.

OXAAL, I. (1967) Black Intellectuals come to Power. Cambridge, Mass.: Schenkman.

RAPOPORT, J. (1971) Small States: Status and Problems. New York: Arno Press.

ROSENBAUM, N. (1970) "Success in foreign policy: the British in Cyprus, 1878-1960." Canadian Journal of Political Science 3, 4: 604-627.

ROSENAU, J. N. [ed.] (1969) Linkage Politics: Essays on the Convergence of National and International Systems. New York: Free Press.

––– (1968) "Moral fervor, systemic analysis and scientific consciousness in foreign policy research," pp. 197-236 in A. Ranney (ed.) Political Science and Public Policy. Chicago: Markham.

––– (1967) "Compatibility, consensus, and an emerging political science of adaptation." Amer. Pol. Sci. Rev. 61, 983-988.

——— (1966) "Pre-theories and theories of foreign policy," pp. 27-92 in R. B. Farrell (ed.) Approaches to Comparative and International Politics. Evanston: Northwestern Univ. Press.

SALMORE, S. A. and C. F. HERMANN (1969) "The effect of size, development and accountability on foreign policy." Peace Research Society Papers, 14, 17-30.

SINGER, J. (1961) "The level of analysis problem in international relations," pp. 77-92 in K. Knorr and S. Verba (eds.) The International System: Essays. New Jersey: Princeton Univ. Press.

SCOLNICK, J. M. Jr. (1972) Observations about Selected Aspects of the Use of Conflict Event Data in Empirical Cross-National Studies of Conflict. Dallas: International Studies Association. (mimeo)

SINGHAM, A. W. (1967) The Hero and the Crowd in the Colonial Polity. New Haven: Yale Univ. Press.

SMALL, M. and J. D. SINGER (1973) "The diplomatic importance of states." World Politics, 15, 4: 577-599.

DE SMITH, S. A. (1970) Microstates and Micronesia: Problems of America's Pacific Islands and Other Minute Territories. New York: New York Univ. Press.

SNYDER, R. C., H. W. BRUCK and B. SAPIN (1954) Decision-Making as an Approach to the Study of International Politics. Princeton Univ.: Foreign Policy Analysis, Series 3.

SPROUT, H. and M. (1968) "The dilemma of rising demands and insufficient resources." World Politics 20, (July): 660-693.

TAYLOR, C. (1969) "Statistical typology of micro-states and territories." Social Science Information 8, 101-17.

——— and M. HUDSON [eds.] (1972) World Handbook of Political and Social Indicators. New Haven: Yale Univ. Press.

United Nations General Assembly Records (1967) Supp. 1.A. U.N. Document A/6701/Add. 1.

VAYRYNEN, R. (1971) "On the definition and measurement of small power status." Cooperation and Conflict, 6, 2: 91-102.

VELLUT, J. (1967) "Small states and the problem of war and peace: some consequences of the emergence of smaller states in Africa." J. of Peace Research 4, 3: 252-269.

VITAL, D. (1967) The Inequality of States. London: Oxford Univ. Press.

YOUNG, O. R. (1968) A Systemic Approach to International Politics. New Jersey: Princeton Univ. Center of International Studies, Research Monograph No. 33.

APPENDIX A

A PROPOSITIONAL INVENTORY OF HYPOTHESES ABOUT MICROSTATE FOREIGN POLICY BEHAVIOR

The objective of this propositional inventory is to present the hypotheses which have been made about microstate foreign policy behavior in summary form. It is hoped that the abstraction of these hypotheses will facilitate students in their efforts to test them against hard data.

1. FOREIGN POLICY ORIENTATIONS

Hypothesis 1.0

Microstates are entities with very limited natural and human resources.

Hypothesis 1.1

The very limited domestic resources of microstates tend to make them heavily dependent on the external environment for support.

Hypothesis 1.1.1

Dependence on the external environment for support makes microstates highly responsive to events which occur abroad.

Hypothesis 1.1.2

Deficiencies in the resources available to the governmental machinery restrict the capacity of microstates to perceive opportunities arising from external events, and respond positively.

Hypothesis 1.2

While microstates are highly dependent on external support to achieve domestic goals, their instrumentalities for manipulating the external environment are severely limited.

2. SCOPE OF MICRO STATE FOREIGN POLICY

Hypothesis 2.0

Microstates demonstrate a very low level of participation in international affairs.

Hypothesis 2.1

The external actions of microstates are narrowly delimited in geographic and functional scope.

Hypothesis 2.2

Microstate external activity is concerned mainly with economic issues.

Hypothesis 2.3

Inter-governmental organizations provide the major arena for microstate external activity.

Hypothesis 2.4

Microstates tend to avoid the use of force as a technique of statecraft.

3. DECISION MAKING PROCESSES AND OUTPUTS

Hypothesis 3.0

Microstate foreign policy decision-making is predominantly an individual rather than a group process.

Hypothesis 3.1

The chief decision maker in the microstate participates actively in the various stages of the decision-making process.

Hypothesis 3.2

Microstate decision-making processes tend to be personalized and authoritarian.

Hypothesis 3.2.1

Personalized and authoritarian decision-making processes are more likely to be found in new microstates which have had a colonial experience than those with a longer tradition of representative government.

Hypothesis 3.2.2

In microstates, decisions on foreign policy are usually made by the head of government even where the formal role of foreign minister is performed by a different individual.

Hypothesis 3.2.3

In many microstates the head of government also acts as his own foreign minister.

Hypothesis 3.3

In attempting to minimize administrative costs the chief foreign policy decision maker may perform multiple roles.

Hypothesis 3.3.1

The performance of multiple roles can give rise to problems of role competition.

Hypothesis 3.3.2

Where domestic and foreign policy roles are performed by the same individual, foreign policy demands may be neglected in favor of domestic demands, particularly if they appear to be less urgent.

Hypothesis 3.3.3

Where domestic opportunities appear to be limited, the decision maker will give disproportionate attention to foreign policy issues.

Hypothesis 3.4

In microstates the supporting bureaucratic structure tends to be weak.

Hypothesis 3.5

The constricted social parameters of microstates give rise to a high intensity of face-to-face interaction, resulting in a polarization of cooperative and conflictual relationships.

Hypothesis 3.5.1

Advice tendered to decision makers will not be regarded as objective nor treated as such.

Hypothesis 3.6

In microstates where political mobilization is based on a charismatic tradition decision makers will place little emphasis on accountability to the public for policy choices.

Hypothesis 3.7

Political parties, legislatures, and public opinion play a minimal role in foreign policy formulation.

Hypothesis 3.8

Manpower and financial resource deficiencies limit the size and the organization of the foreign policy establishment in microstates.

Hypothesis 3.8.1

Very few persons will be involved in the monitoring of international events and occurrences and the execution of foreign policy.

Hypothesis 3.8.2

Microstate foreign ministries tend to be unable to conduct necessary research which should provide the basis for important foreign policy decisions.

Hypothesis 3.8.3

Microstates are restricted in their information and communication networks.

Hypothesis 3.9

Because of their difficulty in interpreting the information which comes from the external environment, microstates will be slow to perceive various opportunities and constraints.

Hypothesis 3.9.1

Microstate foreign policies tend to be reactive rather than active.

4. MICROSTATES AND THE INTERNATIONAL SYSTEM

Hypothesis 4.0

The viability of microstates is more dependent on the existence of systemic phenomena than on capabilities possessed by them.

Hypothesis 4.1

Microstates contribute to the maintenance of stability in the international system, and in international subsystems.

Hypothesis 4.2

Since the activities of microstates comprise a very small part of the total transactions of the international system, actions which infringe system rules are not destabilizing and are therefore permissible.

Hypothesis 4.3

Microstate participation in international affairs is concentrated at two levels: the global system and the contiguous arena.

5. SIZE AND INTERNAL-EXTERNAL INTERDEPENDENCIES

Hypothesis 5.0

Microstate political systems are likely to be highly penetrated.

Hypothesis 5.1

The penetration of microstate political systems results from the shortage of domestic capabilities.

Hypothesis 5.2

The degree of penetration will vary according to the issue which is being processed.

Hypothesis 5.2.1

The greatest degree of penetration is likely to occur in the economic resource issue-area.

APPENDIX B

LIST OF MICROSTATES, SHOWING DATA ON TOTAL LAND AREA, TOTAL POPULATION, POPULATION DENSITY, NATIONAL INCOME, AND NATIONAL INCOME PER CAPITA

STATE	TOTAL LAND AREA (SQ.KM)	ESTIMATED POPULATION IN 1970	POPULATION DENSITY PER SQ.KM.	NATIONAL INCOME (US$M)(DATA FOR LATEST AVAILABLE YEAR)	NATIONAL INCOME PER CAPITA (U.S.$)
The Bahamas	13,935	175,000	13	---	
Bahrien	598	215,000 *	360	---	
Barbados	430	238,000	553	140(1970)	588
Bhutan	47,000	836,000 *	18	40(1963)	
Botswana	600,270	648,000	1	57(1967)	
Congo Brazzaville	342,000	936,000 *	3	145(1963)	
Cyprus	9,251	633,000	68	505(1970)	798
Equatorial Guinea	28,051	290,000 *	10	---	
Fiji	18,160	520,000	28	171(1968)	
Gabon	267,667	500,000	2	344(1970)	
The Gambia	11,295	364,000	32	25(1963)	
Guyana	214,969	714,000	3	219(1969)	688
Iceland	103,000	204,000	2	431(1970)	2,113
Kuwait	16,000	757,000	47	2,?5?(196?)	?,??
Lesotho	30,354	1,043,000	34	71(1967)	
Luxembourg	2,586	339,000	131	735(1969)	2,168
Maldives	298	108,000 *	362	---	
Malta	316	326,000	1,032	205(1969)	
Mauritius	2,096	836,000	399	171(1968)	629
Oman	212,457	657,000	3	45(1963)	
Qatar	22,014	79,000 *	4	---	
Swaziland	17,363	408,000	24	57(1967)	
Tonga	699	86,000	123	---	
Trinidad and Tobago	5,128	945,000	184	696(1968)	
Western Samoa	2,842	143,000	50	---	

* Estimates prepared by United Nations

-- denotes Data not available

Values of National Income per Capita has been calculated where Data on National Income and Population are

GEORGE L. REID is a senior Civil Servant in the Government of Barbados and is currently attached to the Ministry of Finance and Planning. He received his undergraduate education at the University of the West Indies, Jamaica, and did his postgraduate study at the University of Southampton, England, for which he received the Ph.D. degree. He has worked in the Ministry of External Affairs, Barbados, and has represented his country at many regional and international conferences. In 1972 he was a Visiting Research Scholar at the Patterson School of Diplomacy and International Commerce, University of Kentucky. He is currently preparing a study on the relationship between planning and small-state development.